BUSINESS IS EASY

BY

JASON REID

WITH ILLUSTRATIONS
BY
BOBBY ALDERMAN

ISBN-13: 978-1-941768-22-8

Special thanks to my business partners at National Services
Group and CEO Coaching International for letting me be me
all these years. To my wife Kim, my kids, Derek, Ashlyn, Kyle
and Ryan who we lost last year due to suicide at the age of 14.
I love them all with all my heart.

A portion of the proceeds from this book will go to
chooselife.org, a foundation I formed to end Teen Suicide by
the year 2030.

Book design by Bobby Alderman

First Printing, 2019

Printed in China

Waterside Productions
2055 Oxford Ave
Cardiff, CA 92007

waterside.com

This book is dedicated to the entrepreneur who is way too busy and may have just a touch of ADD. It is dedicated to people like me!

INTRODUCTION

If you are like me, you have a stack of business books in your office which you would like to read but don't seem to find the time to read them.

If you are also like me, you wish they were shorter. The concepts are truly common sense, you just need to be reminded of the things you are sometimes not doing.

If you are like me, you don't need to have 15 pages of someone saying the same thing in different ways to remind you of what you are not doing.

If you are like me, you just want your information in short, digestible and memorable chunks.

If you are like me, you are going to love this book! Because, Business Is Easy! We make it not so easy when we are not doing the things we need to... the things that are in the pages of this book.

There is no table of contents on purpose, it is not organized in a specific manner. It is meant for you to open at any page, at any time, read, pause, digest, think about the concept, laugh at the illustration and then go back to work.

Keep it on your desk and enjoy!

- Jay

Trust but verify. One of the biggest mistakes that leaders make is to assign a task and then never ensure that it was done properly. Create "exception report" systems to verify execution.

People are not robots so don't treat them that way. Understand what your people want outside of work and help them achieve it. Not only does this create loyalty, it also creates friends and friends are always there to help each other.

Expect and let people make mistakes; most of us have to learn by doing, not by being told. Sometimes you have to touch the hot stove yourself in order to learn why it's a bad idea. If you touch the hot stove twice though, well, you really can't work here anymore.

Most people don't wake up and go to work hoping to fail. They fail because they did not know what you expected of them. Set high expectations, clearly communicate them, and you'll be pleasantly surprised how people will rise to meet them.

Why do we have the greatest military in the world? That's easy, because the military trains constantly on everything they need to do. Why are many companies substandard in terms of performance? Because they don't invest in training. Train your people for desired results.

Salaries get people to show up and work normal hours. Bonuses for achieving specific and measurable outcomes cause people to stay past 5 pm with a smile on their face. Always smile when you sign bonus and commission checks. Why? Imagine what your business would look like if you had none to sign.

Hire slow and fire fast. Take your time in the hiring process to get to know the people you are bringing on board. And while every new hire makes mistakes, if they are not who they said they were, let them go quickly.

Ask questions and listen! You have two ears and one mouth; pretend you have four ears and one mouth.

Your goal as an interviewer is to go as deep as you can. Every answer to a question should lead you to a new question that helps you peel back the onion and get to who the person really is.

When you have an "A" player in front of you, the interview is reversed, they can go anywhere. Why should they work with you? Practice your "Why my company" speech. Why should anyone come work for you? What makes you special?

Always check references. Do your research including checking LinkedIn, Facebook, Twitter, Instagram, etc. Know who you are calling. Keep digging and the more you keep them talking—the more likely you are to get the real scoop.

Only hire people who are better than you. If you are lucky and smart the people you hire will be better than you at everything. If they are not better than you at everything, at least make sure that they are better than you in what you hired them to do. Never settle, there are plenty of people out there better than you! Remember, if you are the smartest person in the room, you are in the wrong room.

If you believe that you only want to hire "A" players, then the unemployment rate does not matter. "A" players are rarely unemployed. They are working for and coveted by others. Go find them and convince them to come work for you. Remember, there is always some egotistical boss out there who is treating them poorly.

Assuming the candidate has the skills to do the job, ask yourself the most important question—can you see yourself enjoying their company one-on-one for a few hours at a time? If the answer is no, then don't kid yourself, find someone else. Life is too short to cringe every time their number comes across your phone. Only work with people that you like and respect.

Know your numbers. What are the key drivers of revenue?
What drives gross profit? What are your monthly below the
line expenses? Understand all of this and you will understand
what drives your net profit.

If you don't know your revenue and profit for the month off the top of your head, you are not running a business, the business is running you! If you are surprised by your financial statements, you are not running your business, it is running you. Monthly financial statements should only confirm what you already know.

Cash is king! Know your cash level on a daily or weekly basis, whichever is suited for your business. Cash is like gas in your tank and we all know what happens when you run out of gas.

Financials are due on the 15th of the following month at the latest, period, no excuses.

SEPTEMBER
2018
1 2 3
4 5 6 7 8 9 10
11 12 13 14 15 16 17
18 19 20 21 22 23 24
25 26 27 28 29 30

The balance sheet is not just for CFOs and banks. Understand how the profit and loss and balance sheet are related. The bodies are buried in the balance sheet.

No one ever got rich selling dollar bills for 95 cents, except Jeff Bezos. You are not Jeff Bezos.

Figure out how to fly above the fray and be clear on what makes you different than everyone else. If you don't know, how can you expect your customers to?

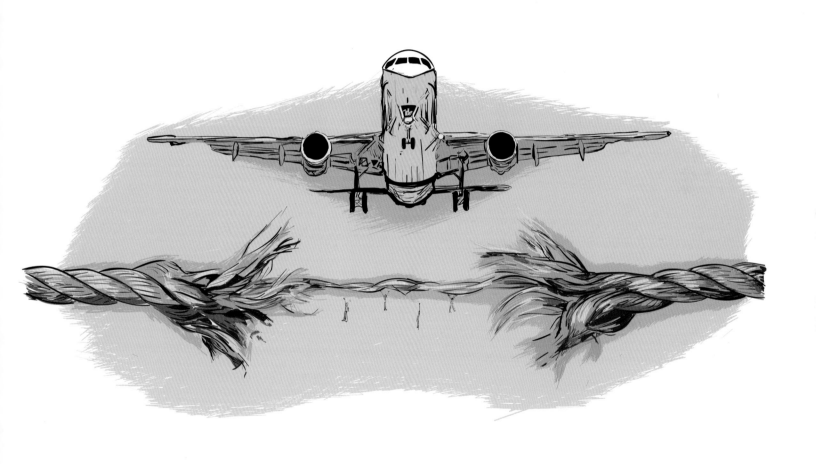

Your job is to steer the ship towards markets with the best margins and least competition.

Understand everything you can about your competition. Who they are. What makes them tick. Who their best people are. What their pricing strategies are. And keep your ear to the ground--sometimes there's great truth in rumors.

Don't stoop to their level, no matter how much you want to. Nothing good ever came from slamming the competition.

Play the imagination game. If you were your competition,
how would you compete against you?

Model the masters. What do the best of the class in your industry do and how do they do it?

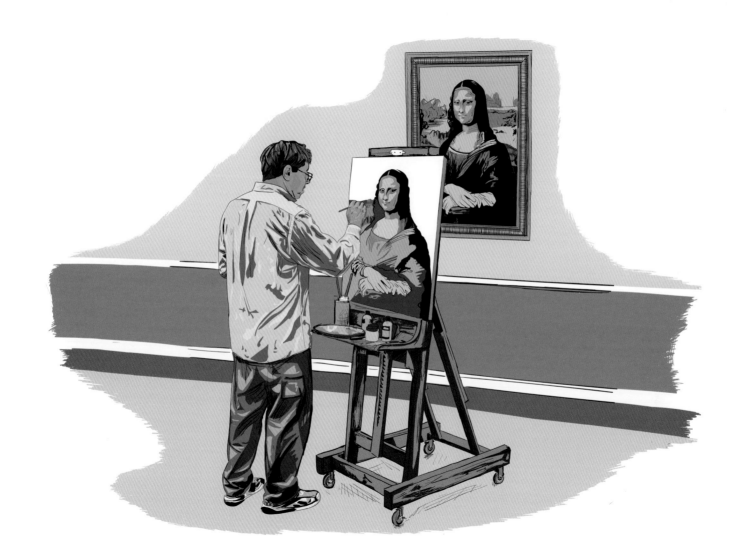

There is no uncharted territory. Someone has been there, done that.
Find out who and learn.

Right now, there is someone in their parent's garage trying to figure out a way to own your industry. They will succeed, are you ready for that moment? Innovate or die.

Your brand is not what you think it is. It's what your customers think of you. Your customers determine your brand. Remember, the most fragile asset your company owns is its BRAND. Treat it with care.

vs.

Don't ignore the Brand Assassins. Yelp, Twitter, Facebook and LinkedIn have the power to destroy your company. Engage the haters, show everyone you care, do your best to solve problems and misunderstandings.

Know what's being said about you. Monitor Facebook, Twitter, LinkedIn, Yelp, Google reviews etc., on a weekly basis.

Understand your cost to acquire a customer. What is it across all of your marketing efforts and what should it be?

When it comes to marketing, TEST, TEST, TEST, and when you have a winner, bet BIG.

It's easier to sell more stuff to existing customers than to find new customers. If you have a 50% or greater concentration of your business with a few customers, ignore this rule and go find more customers.

An unmanaged sales person is like an unbridled horse;
they will take you places you don't want to go.

Sales people are like pack animals, they need to be among their own kind to survive and thrive. Alone they will wither and die, and they may take your company with them. Hire more sales people!

Sales and operations will never completely understand each other, and they don't need to. They just need to get along without coming to blows. If sales and operations get along perfectly, then you are not pushing sales hard enough.

Be aware the ether of the well-groomed sales person. Don't hire just for looks, smiles, and personality. Dig deep in the interview and figure out what they have accomplished in their lives. Remember, they sell for a living and an interview is just another sales opportunity.

Managing sales people is all about managing activity. What activities do your sales people need to be doing on a daily and weekly basis in order to increase sales? Understand what these specific activities are and measure them! Sales people who call this "micro-management" are the ones who are not doing the key activities. Your best sales people will be excited to show you how hard they work!

Often times, the best decision you can make is to walk or run away from a deal. Focus on selling what you are capable of delivering at an acceptable profit.

CPAs have seen hundreds of business owners and the mistakes they make. They should be a trusted advisor not just someone you call at tax time.

Don't just get advice from one lawyer or accountant. Getting a "second" opinion is not just for doctors. It's for accountants and lawyers, too.

All of the great players have a coach, so do all the great CEO's.
Get one or you'll be outfoxed by those who do.

The right bank is the best partner you can ever have. Share your vision, your ups and downs. Great banks can handle good news and bad news, just not no news. Get ahead of the curve. Be transparent.

No one ever regretted getting lots of different opinions on how to solve a problem. Reach out and talk to everyone! Discern, sift, then decide.

You can't be a fast growth entrepreneur and a perfectionist, pick one. Creation is messy. If you choose perfectionist, be satisfied with slow growth, really, really slow growth.

Don't try to be everything to everybody. Try to be the best solution or product for a large enough niche to cash in. Know your special sauce and where you fit in.

Beware the robots, they are real and they are coming after you!

As we say at CEO Coaching International, set Huge Outrageous Targets because no one achieves BIG by thinking small.

Plan yearly and quarterly, review weekly, and execute daily! Five-year plans are for Apple and companies that existed 15 years ago. The speed of change has made three- and five-year plans obsolete—even for Apple.

If you don't have a destination in mind, you will never get there.
Set your compass.

Set it and forget it is not a management strategy.
It's a hurricane barreling toward you.

Success cannot exist without passion. On a scale of 1 to 10, what is your level of passion for what you are doing right now? Think about it...then do something about it.

The best person to do the task may not be you or even exist in your company. Outsource to a pro!

BUSINESS

MORTGAGE SOLUTIONS!
We provide complete Property Management, Leasing and Real Estate Services for Residential and Commercial Properties.

ATTENTION: HOME OWNER
2 bedrooms Property has been completely renovated and is currently occupied!! Both tenants are currently on leases and each unit is rented at $400

EXCELLENT INVESTMENT
2 Family (DUPLEX)- Both units have 2 bedrooms and 1 bath. Property has been completely renovated and is currently occupied. Both tenants are occup... ...s and each unit is cu... ...00 and $450.

...AL LOANS
...applications on ...property types; ...ly construction ...ntres

...Use

...MONEY DOWN
...help home buyers to purchase ...eir home with **ZERO** money ...own. call us today to put together a proposal for an offer on your property.

OFFICE AVAILABLE
8 individual enclosed office space cubicles (with desks) at a great location. Use of Boardrooms and general facilities. General Parking nearby. 275$ /each
...M. DOWATONA

CAREERS

GENERAL HELP WANTED
Seeking someone for general help. eg. filing, organizing, errands, answering emails. Must know how to type. $10 per hour to start

★ ★ ★ ★ ★

WEEKEND RECEPTION
We are seeking a general office assistant for Sunday afternoons between the hours of 11:30am to 5:00pm. $12/H

NEW AD

BOOK ILLUSTRATER
Our client is seeking a talented and experienced illustrator to join their team for a short-term project illustrating the fundamentals of business.

Medical Assistant Training
Online Classes We want you to be successful. Just click the link

★ CALL NOW ★

Sales Assistant
We currently have an excellent opportunity in our sales office. For more information about the company. See our website or send resume.

TUTORS NEEDED
We are looking for: highly skilled, motivated and dynamic individuals who have strong communication skills. Candidate must possess a love for teaching. $12/n

When you screw up, realize it, own it, accept it, and communicate it.

THAT'S MY FAULT

What are the key metrics that drive your business? What happens when you understand them, track them, and make them happen? How do you move them and what happens when you do? Remember, what gets measured gets done.

Being an entrepreneur means you may end up working 80 instead of 40 hours for less than you make at 40 hours with more risk than you expected. If that scares you then don't kid yourself, it's not for you.

They don't teach failure at MBA school, yet you don't succeed until you understand how to fail. Just don't make failure a habit.

It's impossible to multi-task. What is possible is to flip back and forth between tasks without letting the last task interfere with the one you are on. This is a learned skill.

Be a lifelong learner. When you get your 1st degree black belt, the 7th degrees will tell you congrats, you just graduated kindergarten. Your business education does not stop at your bachelors, or MBA. If you are not committed to learning, you are not committed to success. What are you doing to commit to life-long learning?

There are 168 hours in a week. Understand how you truly spend them. Track your time for a month in 15-minute increments and understand where the opportunities are. Many people say they work 80-hour weeks. That would be 6 am to 10 pm Monday to Friday not including breaks, lunch, and drive time. How many hours do you really work?

Flying at 30,000 feet going 500 miles an hour is awesome! The problem is you can't see what's happening on the ground. Get your head out of the clouds and go talk to your employees and customers.

You are the average of the five people you spend the most time with.
Are you scared?

All cars and people have blind spots.
If you don't know yours, you are going to crash.

Sometimes, change is a threshold of pain thing. When the pain becomes unbearable, you will change. Lower your pain tolerance!

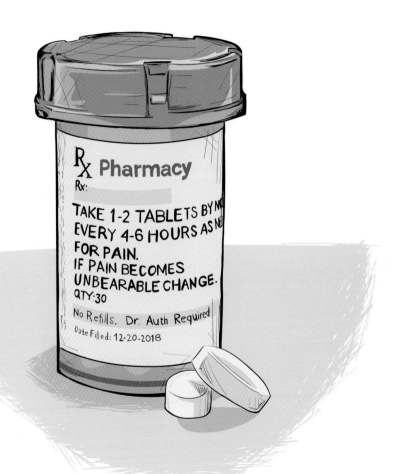

Don't believe your own press--remember you wrote it!

That nagging voice in your head is rarely right. That voice coming from your gut, though, is rarely wrong.

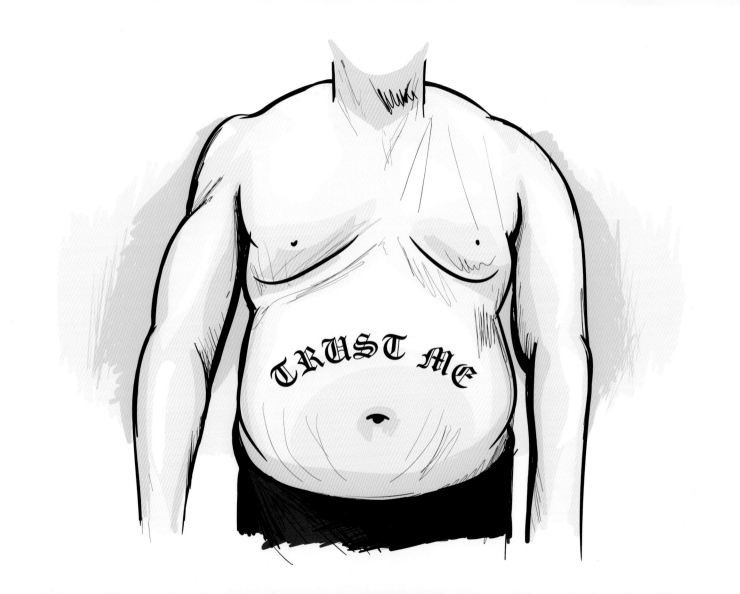

Partnerships are like marriages, they take time, effort, and nurturing to succeed. Likewise, partnership failure is just as messy and expensive as a divorce.

That book about your life story, no one cares. Well, maybe your spouse does. On second thought, they don't care either.

No one ever wins in court. Settle your lawsuits and cut your losses. Unless you feel bad for the poor lawyers.

Beware the marginal opportunity; it is shiny and new and wants to suck away your time and money.

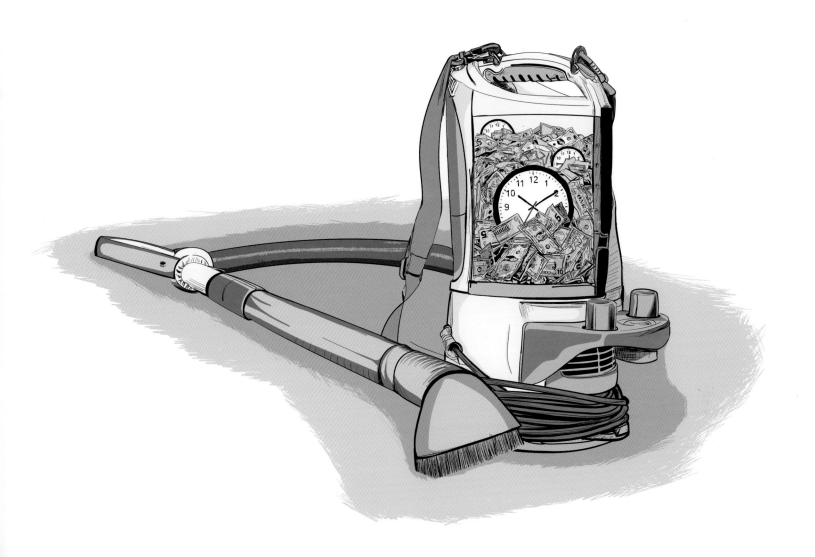

Money comes and money goes, but time only goes.
Remember what's important in life.

You live in a fishbowl and everyone is watching you. Every action is being questioned so don't be an ass when you screw up. Don't justify it, own it. Your employees and kids will remember the smallest comment you made five years ago that you forgot about. Think before you speak.

You can always spot a startup that's about to fail by visiting their work space. The nicer it is, the more organized it is, the more likely it is to fail. Focus on driving revenue and profits, then buy yourself a nice desk.

You can't accomplish 10 things this quarter.
Pick your top three and make them happen. Stat.

Things

1 2 3 4 5
6 7 8 9 10

Dream BIG, execute in reality, bask in the outcome.

Remember that system and process you put in place last year? Someone has modified it without asking. Now's the time to go check on it.

A fish doesn't stink from the head down. It stinks everywhere.

Yes, "pioneers get the arrows" has been true since the dawn of time. Nothing has changed and history repeats itself, or at least rhymes. Take the arrows.

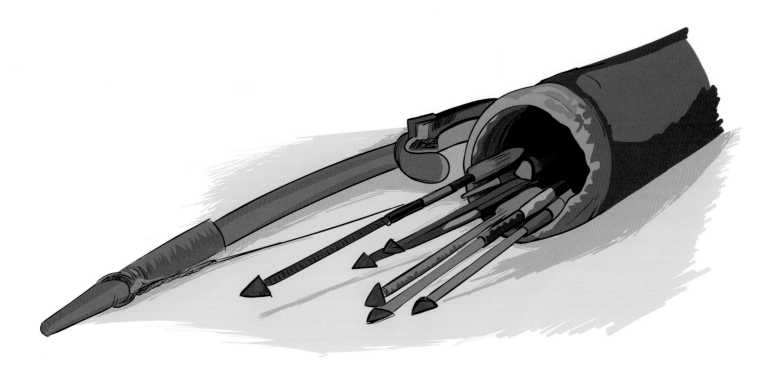

As your company grows, not everyone will grow at the same speed. Some will fail to keep up. But by investing in their education along the way, more will make the journey with you. If you don't invest in your people, you are doomed to be continually replacing your management team.

Managing any project, no matter how big or small, is always the same. Each team member needs to understand their role, and what they need to accomplish each day by 10am, 12pm, 2pm, and 4pm in order for the project to be on track and succeed. This process applies to construction projects, to software projects, and to everything in between.

Meetings are a time suck, purposely trim 25% off the time set for every meeting you go into and get back a huge chunk of your day.

In life and business, it's not what you do, it's who you do it with.
Choose wisely.

Meditate. Regardless of method or style, meditation is about awareness. Stop for a second and take stock of your goals, your intentions, your current activity. Gain awareness of what's important, what's working, what needs to change. It's hard to adjust mid-air.

Fail Fast!!!! The FastTrack to Success has many of these Pit Stops along the way.

People forget everything you say, but remember everything you do. Talk about your values, but communicate them through your actions if you want your team to act on them.

ACTIONS > WORDS

What is your emotional recovery rate? How long does it take you to bounce back from failure. The best entrepreneurs have very quick recovery times.

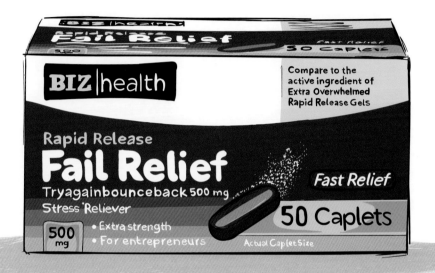

Create bonus and incentive plans that actually incentivize a specific behavior. If the bonus is tied to the overall health of the company, it will have ZERO effect on behavior.

Always include a meal or a drink when evaluating top talent. Non-verbal cues, menu choices and attitude towards servers may give you very valuable insight.

The greatest gift we can give someone is our attention.

Praised behavior gets repeated. Don't underestimate the power of praise, whether through a short phone call, conversation or handwritten card. Done right, those gestures are remembered long after the bonus check is spent.

You haven't failed until you quit trying.

Your stop doing list is more important than your to do list.

LEARN through the Socratic method, quiz others to find the answers that you need.

The truth is in the numbers. Everything else is an opinion or perception.

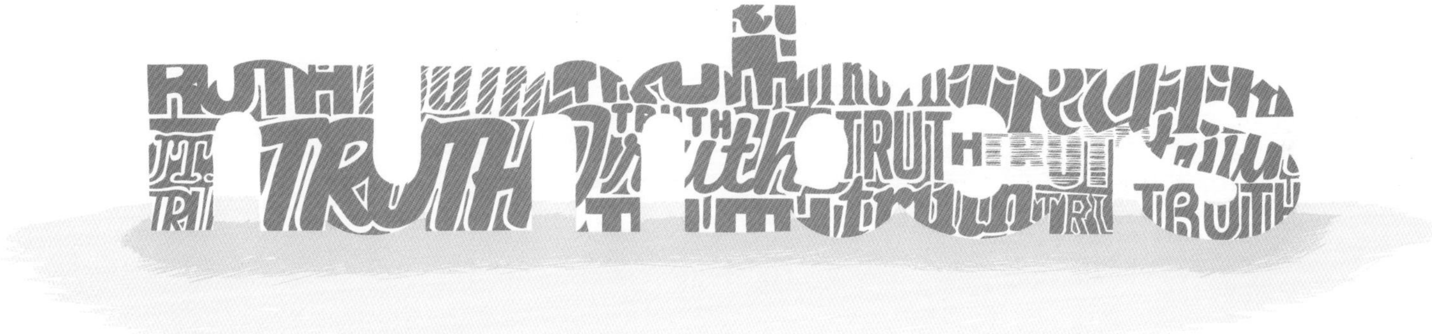
numbers

Know your people. What do they do when they aren't at work? What's important to them? What keeps them awake at night? What are their greatest aspirations? When you're a part of their solution set and a vehicle to their goals, they will crawl through glass for you.

Some with simmering paranoia make the best sales people. They are always thinking the deal is not going to happen and they take all the right steps to make sure to get the close.

Practice Authentic Leadership – Be the same person at home, at work and with your friends, everyone knows when you are not.

Be a truth giver and a truth receiver.

Integrity means do what you say you are going to do...on time..every time. If you don't, how can you hold your employees to the same standard?

Know your MTP – Your Massive Transformational Purpose